道德經

TAO TE CHING

the book of the way and its power

a new translation

by

JOHN R. MABRY

the apocryphile press
BERKELEY, CA
www.apocryphile.org

apocryphile press
BERKELEY, CA

Apocryphile Press
1700 Shattuck Ave #81
Berkeley, CA 94709
www.apocryphile.org

Illustrations by Jim Hardesty

ISBN 9781955821339

Contents

Introduction

The *Tao Te Ching* is a book of Chinese philosophical poetry, written sometime between the seventh and the fourth centuries BCE. According to tradition it was written by a quiet librarian named Lao Tzu, which in Chinese can mean, curiously enough, either Old Man or Old Child. Lao Tzu was said to be a contemporary of Confucius, although many years his senior, and the legend of their ideological rivalry is very popular.

Scholars nowadays doubt the historicity of the person Lao Tzu and many believe that the *Tao Te Ching*, the book attributed to him, to be a composite work collected by an early Taoist school, much the same way that Jews and Christians today doubt whether Moses actually wrote the *Torah*. Whether Lao Tzu wrote every word of the *Tao Te Ching* is unimportant—most probably he is the founder of a school, the teachings of which are best represented by this book. He is, nonetheless, its traditional author, and for the purposes of this introduction, we will give him the credit.

In the *Tao Te Ching* we encounter a form of nature mysticism, but it is a unique and amazing form. As in other nature religions, in Taoism humans are not separate from nor dominant over nature. We are a part of nature. The Taoist sees him or herself as equal to all other things in Creation, and in fact, it is from observing nature that wisdom is gleaned. There is no divine revelation in Taoism. Nature reveals everything we need to know, if only we have the eyes—and the patience—to see it. Nature, in Taoism, is always correct and has the answers to every problem. Humans think too much and that gets us into trouble.

So what is the Tao? This is a difficult question, and Lao Tzu tells us right off in his first poem in the *Tao Te Ching* that "the Tao that can be described in words is not the true Tao." Like most mystics, however, he does not let the impossibility of his task deter him, and spends the next 80 poems trying to do just that. We are used to thinking of divinity in terms of God or the gods, but Taoism demands a very different orientation. The Tao is not a god, ruling over subjects, or weilding power over nature—the Tao is a part of Nature, or more accurately, nature is a part of the Tao, and therefore the Tao is not a separate personality, like the gods. The Tao is impersonal. The sparrow does not perceive divinity as a personality but as the very web of being in which it moves and of which it consists. The Taoist follows the example of the animals and the Earth herself, and perceives of the divine in the same way.

The Tao is simply that which *is*. By observing nature we can discern certain characteristics about it, and also discern healthier ways of being human as well. There is no one to pray to in Taoism, there are no rites to be performed, no liturgy to be recited. There is simply the world as-it-is, and we will either find our proper place within it or we will suffer.

According to Lao Tzu, all things in nature are in balance. The Tao consists of both Yin and Yang, opposing forces that define and sustain each other: good and bad, light and dark, matter and spirit. The *Tao Te Ching* speaks of matter and spirit as if they were partners, one incapable of functioning without the other. Taoists speak of spirit as "non-being," implying something that exists in objective reality, but which possesses no physical manifestation, or "being." This unitive vision of spirituality is difficult for Westerners reared with pervasive dualism. Lao Tzu asks, as if speaking directly to us, "Being both body and spirit, can you embrace unity and not be fragmented?" (Poem 10).

To illustrate his vision, Lao Tzu presents non-being as absolutely necessary for physical realities to "function," and vice versa, saying, "Thirty spokes join together at one hub, but it is the hole in the center that makes it operable. Clay is molded into a pot, but it is the emptiness inside that makes it useful. Doors and windows are cut to make a room, but it is the empty spaces that we use" (Poem 11).

The first time I read these verses, chills ran down my spine. I felt that I had been told a great secret that was the most obvious thing in the world: in the relationship between matter and spirit, one is not dominant. "Existence and non-existence produce one another." Lao Tzu explains, "Existence is what we have, but non-existence is what we use."

In addition to non-being, which is *thing*, or noun-oriented, Lao Tzu also offers a matching concept which is *action*, or verb-oriented: non-action. The Chinese word for non-action is *wu-wei*. *Wu-wei* literally means "not doing," but it has many applications.

With this concept, Lao Tzu speaks directly to contemporary westerners and our fast-paced culture. He tells us, "If you spend your life filling your senses and rushing around 'doing' things, you will be beyond hope." It is difficult for some of us to slow down and not feel guilty.

Instead, Lao Tzu asks, "When Heaven gives and takes away, can you be content to just let things come or go? And even when you understand all things, can you simply allow yourself to be?" (Poem 10).

Slowing down enough to hear the voice of the divine, or to observe the Way of the Tao, is, in my experience, one of the most important spiritual disciplines of all. An old joke reminds us that while Westerners say, "Don't just sit there, do something!", Eastern wisdom says, "Don't just do something, sit there!" The value of not-doing is every bit as great as the value of non-being, or spirit, and the health of our non-being/spirit is utterly dependent upon our ability to not-do.

In the *Tao Te Ching* Lao Tzu also concerns himself greatly with leadership, both political and spiritual. There is a tradition that the *Tao Te Ching* was originally written as a guide for a young ruler on how to rule well. Lao Tzu's advice is about as counter-intuitive as we in the West can imagine.

"Loving all people and leading them well," he asks, "can you do this without imposing your will?" This is a great and important question for us, who are surrounded by traditions notorious for spiritual coercion. Unfortunately, we often unwittingly perpetuate the cycle of coercion. But Taoism suggests that, like water, all things simply flow out and return, void of any notions of "right" or "wrong."

The key to being successful in spiritual leadership, according to Lao Tzu, is to *not try*. "Therefore the sage, not trying, cannot fail," says Lao Tzu. "Not clutching, she cannot lose." Likewise in our own spiritual lives,

"the truly good person does not try to be good."
Goodness needs to come naturally, effortlessly, like
breathing or hearing. The sage is not concerned with
being good. He or she does not give it a thought. It is
not a goal. The goal is to respond humanely—as a
human would—to whatever situation life gives.

Taoism has a very different conception of sin than
we are used to in the west. "Sin" in Taoism is not about
doing evil or disobeying authority, instead it is simply
going against the grain, and one's punishment is imme-
diate and in this world: a life of stress and struggle.
"Salvation" on the other hand, is simply going with the
flow, finding a life of freedom and security, because one
knows how the universe works and can cooperate with
it. There is no "guilt" language in the *Tao Te Ching*. The
Tao's love is universal and unconditional. It is not for
the enlightened only, or the holy or even the moral.
The Tao is there for all. "It is the good person's treasure," Lao Tzu writes, "and the bad person's refuge...
Why did the sages of old value the Tao so much?
Because when you seek, you find. And when you sin,
you are forgiven." How healthy is that?

In Lao Tzu's philosophy, success comes not from
achievement or from the accumulation of spiritual
merit or power. Instead, success is measured by one's
ability to simply be, free of stress, free of striving, free
of conceptions of what one "should be" that is in any
way at odds with how one simply is.

Legend tells us that Lao Tzu, in his old age, finally gave up on trying to teach humanity anything, and gave up on us as a lost cause. He packed his yak, and headed for the wilderness where things were sane. At the top of a mountain pass, the last outpost of civilization, the gatekeeper persuaded Lao Tzu to commit his philosophy to paper before he left humankind forever.

The human race will be forever indebted to the foresight of this gatekeeper, as Lao Tzu's book, consisting of just 5,000 characters, is one of the most sublime, meaningful, and downright practical works of mysticism in the human canon.

—*John R. Mabry*

TAO TE CHING

道可道
非常道
名可名
非常名

1

The Tao that can be described in words is not the true Tao
The Name that can be named is not the true Name.

From non-existence were called Heaven and Earth
From existence all things were born.

In being without desires, you experience the wonder
But by having desires, you experience the journey.
Yet both spring from the same source and differ mostly
   in name.

> This source is called "Mystery"
> Mystery upon Mystery,
> The womb giving birth to all of being.

2

When people see beauty as beautiful,
They recognize other things as ugly.

When people see goodness as good,
They recognize other things as being bad.

Therefore existence and non-existence produce one another
        Difficult and easy achieve each other
        Long and short define each other
        High and low rely on each other
Voice and accompaniment harmonize with one another
Front and back follow each other.

Therefore, the Sage acts without "doing"
And teaches without words.
        All things arise and she does not refuse them.
        She creates, but does not possess
        Accomplishes, but takes no credit
        When finished, she doesn't dwell on it.
Because she does not dwell on it, it is always present.

3

Do not exalt people who are extraordinarily talented
Or the people will become competitive.

> Do not value precious goods
> Or the people will become thieves.

Do not make a public display of riches and finery
Or the people's hearts will be envious and discontent.

Therefore, the wise leader will empty their hearts of coveting
and fill their bellies with sustenance.
> He discourages their ambition
> and strengthens their bones.
If the people are simple and free from desire,
the crafty will not dare to take advantage of them.

By practicing "not doing," nothing will remain undone.

4

The Tao is like an empty pitcher,
Poured from, but never drained.
Infinitely deep, it is the source of all things.

It blunts the sharp,
Unties the knotted,
Shades the bright,
Unites with all dust.

Dimly seen, yet eternally present,
I do not know who gave birth to it,
It is older than any conception of God.

5

Heaven and Earth are impartial,
They allow things to die.

The Sage is not sentimental,
She knows that all beings must pass away.

The space between Heaven and Earth is like a bellows
Empty, yet inexhaustible
The more it is used, the more it produces.

Trying to explain it will only exhaust you.
It is better to hold on to paradox.

6

The spirit of emptiness is eternal.
It is called "the Mysterious Woman."

Her womb is called "the Source of Heaven and Earth."

Dimly seen, yet eternally present
It is always there for you to use. It's easy!

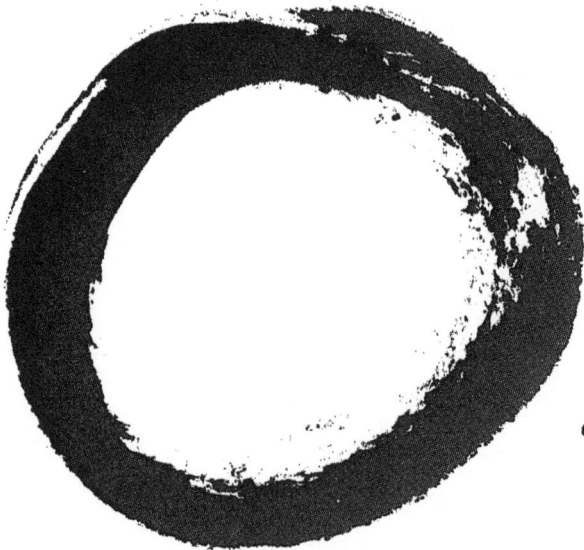

7

Heaven is eternal, and Earth is long-lasting.
Why are they so enduring?
Because they do not live for themselves.

Therefore the Sage puts himself last
And finds himself in the foremost place.
He does not promote himself, thus he is preserved.

Because he has no thought of "self,"
He is perfectly fulfilled.

8

The sagely person is like water
Water benefits all things and does not compete with them.
It gathers in unpopular places.
In this it is like the Tao.

> In dwelling, live close to the Earth.
>
> In thinking, be open to new ideas.
>
> In relationships, be kind.
>
> In speech, tell the truth and keep your word.
>
> In leading people, demonstrate integrity.
>
> In daily matters, be competent.
>
> In acting, consider the appropriate timing.

If you do not try to prove yourself superior to others,
You will be beyond reproach.

9

Filling your cup until it overflows
is not as good as stopping in time.

Oversharpen your sword
and it will not protect you very long.

You may fill your halls with gold and jewels
but you cannot keep them safe.

Being rich, highly esteemed and proud
will only bring you trouble.

When you have done a good job, rest.
This is the Way of Heaven.

10

Being both body and spirit,
can you embrace unity and not be fragmented?
Being spiritually focused,
can you become soft, like a newborn baby?
Being clear in mind and vision,
can you eliminate your flaws?
Loving all people and leading them well,
can you do this without imposing your will?
When Heaven gives and takes away,
can you be content to just let things come or go?
And even when you understand all things,
can you simply allow yourself to *be*?

To give birth and nourish,
To make and not own,
To act but not expect something in return,
To grow, yet not demand this of others,
This is the virtue of Mystery.

11

Thirty spokes join together at one hub,
But it is the hole in the center that makes it operable.

Clay is molded into a pot,
But it is the emptiness inside that makes it useful.

Doors and windows are cut to make a room,
It is the empty spaces that we use.

Therefore, existence is what we have,
But non-existence is what we use.

12

Too many colors tax people's vision.

Too many sounds deaden people's hearing.

Too many flavors spoil people's taste.

Thrill-seeking leads people to do crazy things.

The pursuit of wealth just gets in people's way.

Therefore, the Sage provides for her needs,
not her desires.

She renounces the latter, and chooses the former.

13

Success is often as unsettling as failure.

The world's troubles are no more important
than the well-being of your own body.

Why do I say, "Success is often as unsettling as failure?"

> Success strikes us deep.
> It shakes us up to get it.
> It shakes us up to lose it.

Thus, success is really little different than failure,
for both are unsettling.

Why do I say, "The World's greatest troubles are no more
important than the well-being of your own body?"

> The reason I think I have troubles
> is because I have material existence.
> If I had no body, what troubles
> could I possibly have?

What we must do is see the whole world as our "Self."
Only then will we be worthy
of being entrusted with the World.

Only One who values the World as his own body
can truly rely on the World in return.

14

Look for it and it cannot be seen—it is beyond sight.

Listen for it and it cannot be heard—it is beyond hearing.

Grasp at it and it cannot be caught—it is beyond substance.

These three cannot be fully comprehended.

They are fundamentally connected and somehow they are one.

> Its highest isn't bright.
> Its lowest isn't dark.
> It is infinite!

Continually emerging, completely beyond description,
It returns again and again to nothingness.

And this is what nothingness looks like:
It is the image of the absence of being.
(It sounds vague and elusive to me!)

Approach it and you will not see its beginning
Follow it and you will not see its end.

If you cling to the Tao of ancient times
the present will be no problem.
To know the ancient origin is to follow the Tao.

15

The Sages of old were scholars who knew well
the way of subtlety, mystery and discernment.

Their wisdom was beyond comprehension.
Because they were beyond comprehension,
I can only describe their appearance:

They were cautious, as if crossing a river in winter.
They were hesitant, as if fearing danger from all sides,

They were polite, as if they were guests.

They were always growing,
like the puddle from a melting cube of ice.

They were genuine, like an uncarved block of wood.

They were as open-minded as a valley.

They were open to infinite possibilities, like a turbulent storm.

Who can wait for the storm to stop,
to find peace in the calm that follows?

The person who is able to wait patiently in this peace
will eventually know what is right.
Those who respect the Tao do not go to extremes.
Not going to extremes, they are inconspicuous and content.

16

If you can empty yourself of everything,
you will have lasting peace.
Things arise, but I contemplate their return.
Things flourish and grow, and then return to their Source.
To return to the Source is to know perfect peace.
I call this a return to Life.

Returning to Life is a Universal Constant.
Knowing this is illuminating.
Someone who doesn't understand this is in error
and may act dangerously.

But knowing this Constant, you can embrace all things.
Embracing all things, you can treat them fairly.
Treating them fairly, you are noble.
Being noble, you are like the cosmos.
If you are like the cosmos, you are like the Tao.

If you are like the Tao, you will have eternal life,
and you needn't be afraid of dying.

17

The best leader is one that the people are barely aware of.
The next best is one who is loved and praised by the people.
Next comes one who is feared.
Worst is one who is despised.

If the leader does not have enough faith in the people,
They will not have faith in him.

The best leader puts great value in words and says little
So that when his work is finished
The people all say, "We did it ourselves!"

18

When the great Tao is abandoned,
Ideas of "humanitarianism" and "righteousness" appear.
When intellectualism arises
It is accompanied by great hypocrisy.

When there is strife within a family
Ideas of "brotherly love" appear.

When a nation is plunged into chaos
Politicians become "patriotic."

19

Forget "holiness," abandon "intelligence"
and people will be a hundred times better off.

Give up "humanitarianism," put away "righteousness"
and people will rediscover brotherly love and kindness.

Forget "great art," throw away "profit"
and there will be no more thieves.

These things are superficial and are simply not enough.
People need something solid to hold on to.
And here it is:

> Be real.
> Embrace simplicity.
> Put others first.
> Desire little.

20

Forget ambitious acquisition of knowledge,
and your sorrows will end.
How much difference is there between "yes" and "no"?
What is the distinction between "good" and "evil"?
Must I value what others value? Nonsense!
Having no end to their desires, they are desolate.

People rush here and there, maybe going to a feast,
or perhaps climbing a tower in the springtime.
I alone am calm and unconcerned.
Like an unselfconscious infant
At peace and having no destination.

Most people have more than they need.
But I alone seem lost and out of place.
I have the mind of a fool—so confused!

Ordinary people are bright.
I alone seem dim.
Ordinary people are discriminating.
I alone am ambivalent.

> As quiet as the ocean.
> As free as the wind.

People rush about on their very important business.
But I alone seem incorrigible and uncouth.
I am different from ordinary people;
I enjoy feeding from the Great Mother's breasts.

21

The only virtue worth having is that of following the Tao,
and the only thing you can say about the Tao,
is that it is elusive and evasive.

It is elusive and evasive, yet it can be observed.
It is evasive and elusive, yet it does manifest itself.
It is dim and dark, yet its essence can be grasped.

>Its essence is unquestionably genuine.
>You can put your faith in it.

From the beginning of time until the present,
its Name has remained.
In it one can see all of Creation.
How do I know where all of Creation comes from?
I know the Tao!

22

If you don't want to be broken, bend.
If you want to be straight, allow some crookedness.
If you want to be filled, become empty.
If you want to be made new, let yourself be used.
If you want to be rich, desire little.
Wanting more and more is craziness!

Therefore the Sage embraces oneness
and becomes a model for the world.
Not self-centered, she is enlightened.
Not self-righteous, she is a shining example.
Not self-glorifying, she accomplishes glorious things.
Not boastful, she grows large inside.
She alone does not compete,
And so the world can never overcome her.

When the ancients said, "If you don't want to be broken, bend"
Were they just uttering empty words?
Bend sincerely and wholeness will return to you.

23

Nature uses few words.
So, a whirlwind will not last all morning.
A sudden storm will not last all day.
What causes these?
Heaven and Earth.
If Heaven and Earth need not speak for long,
How much less should humankind?

Therefore, one who seeks the Tao is at one with the Tao.
One who seeks goodness is good.
One who seeks loss is lost.

If you are one with the Tao, the Tao eagerly accepts you.
If you are one with goodness,
goodness is happy to receive you.
If you are one with loss, loss welcomes you.

If you do not trust enough, you will not find trust.

24

One who stands on tiptoe does not stand firm.
One who rushes ahead is likely to trip.
One who listens only to himself cannot learn.
One who considers himself righteous, isn't.
One who brags has nothing to brag about.
One who feels sorry for himself does not grow.

Compared to the Tao, these people are table scraps
and wasted effort,
and not well-liked by anyone or anything.

So, if you follow the Tao, you will not live like that.

風蘭

25

Before Heaven and Earth were born
There was something undescribable.
Perfectly still, having no form,
It stands alone, and does not change.
It acts perpetually, yet never tires.
It could very well be the Mother of the Universe.
I don't know its name, so I just call it the Tao.
If forced to give it a name, I would call it Great.

> Being Great, I call it eternal.
> Being eternal, I call it infinite.
> Being infinite, I call it Reconciliation.

> Therefore, the Tao is Great.
> Heaven is Great.
> The Earth is Great.
> Humankind is also Great.
In the Universe there are these four things which are Great,
And Humankind is one of them.

> Humankind follows the Earth,
> The Earth follows Heaven,
> Heaven follows the Tao,
> And the Tao just acts like itself.

26

Heaviness is the root of lightness.
Stillness is the master of restlessness.

Therefore, the Sage walks all day
and never parts from the baggage wagon.
Although there are many beautiful palaces to behold,
He is beyond such things and is at peace.

Why should the ruler of ten thousand chariots
Act with such frivolity in this world?
To act lightly is to lose one's root.
To be restless is to lose one's self-control.

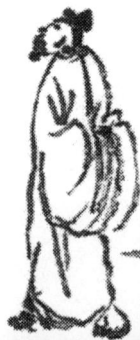

27

A skillful walker leaves no tracks.
A skillful speaker makes no mistakes.
A skillful accountant needs no counting-devices.
A well-made door needs no lock, yet cannot be opened.
A well-made binding uses no rope, yet will not be undone.

> Therefore, the Sage is always there to help people
> So that no one is forsaken.
> She is always there to see to things
> So that nothing is lost.
> This is called being clothed in light.

What is a good person but a bad person's teacher?
What is a bad person but raw material for a good person?

If you do not respect your Teacher,
Or love your "raw material,"
You are greatly confused, regardless of your intelligence.

I call this an essential, yet subtle mystery.

28

Know the active, the masculine
Yet keep to the passive, the feminine
And you will cradle the World.
If you lovingly hold the World
You will know eternal goodness
And will become again as a little child.

Be aware of the obvious—the light
But keep to the mysterious—the dark
And set an example for the world.
Be an example for the world
And do not stray from your calling
And you will return to the Eternal.

Know honor, yet remain humble
And be empty of the world.
Being empty of the world is good enough
And you will return to the simplicity of the uncarved block.
If the block is carved it is trapped in one form and critiqued.
The Sage prefers simplicity and so is ahead of them all.
He knows better than to divide the whole.

29

Do you want to own the World and improve it?

I don't think you can.

You see, the World is sacred.
It can't be improved upon.
If you try you will ruin it.
If you try to own it,
You will lose it.

Therefore, sometimes you must lead and sometimes
you must follow.
Sometimes you need to blow hard, and sometimes you
can breathe easily.
Sometimes you must be strong and sometimes tender.
Sometimes you win and sometimes you lose.

Knowing this, the Sage avoids extremes,
extravagances and exhaustion.

30

A leader who is advised to rely on the Tao
Does not enforce his will upon the world by military means.
For such things are likely to rebound.

> Wherever armies have camped
> Thistles and briars grow.
> In the wake of war
> Bad years are sure to follow.

A good leader accomplishes only what he has set out to do
And is careful not to overestimate his ability.

He achieves his goal, but does not brag.
He effects his purpose, but does not show off.
He is resolute, but not arrogant.
He does what he must, though he may have little choice.
He gets results, but not by force.

Things that grow strong soon grow weak.
This is not the Way of the Tao.
Not following the Tao leads to an early end.

31

All weapons are bad news
And all creatures should detest them.
So those who follow the Tao do not keep them.

(Wise people prefer the left side as the place of honor,
but the General always stands on the right.)

Weapons are the tools of fear.
They are not appropriate for a Sage
And should only be one's last resort.
Peace is always far superior.

There is no beauty in victory.
To find beauty in it would be to rejoice at killing people.
Anyone who delights in slaughter will never find
satisfaction in this world.

(When celebrating happy occasions,
   the left side is the place of honor,
But on unhappy occasions, the right is preferred.
Then we see those of lower rank standing on the left;
The General is given the right-hand position.)

Military officers should observe their duties gravely,
For when many people are killed
They should be mourned with great sorrow.
Celebrate your victory only with funeral rites.

32

The Tao will always be beyond comprehension.
Although it seems trivial
No one in all the world can control it.

If governments and leaders can abide in it
All beings shall gratefully behave likewise.
We would have a Heaven on Earth
And sweet rains would fall.
The people would not need to be told,
They would just naturally do what is right.

When you organize, you must of necessity
use names and order.
But given that, you must also know where to leave off
naming and structuring.
Knowing when to stop, you can avoid danger.
All the World is to the Tao
As rivers flowing home to the sea.

33

One who knows others is intelligent.
One who knows himself is truly wise.

One who overcomes others has force.
One who overcomes the self has true strength.

One who knows he has enough is truly wealthy.
One who has discipline is sincere.
One who remembers his Source will endure.
He embraces death and so does not perish
but lives forever.

34

The great Tao flows everywhere,
to the left and to the right.
All things rely on it for their life
and it does not refuse them.
When its work is done, it does not demand recognition.
It clothes and nourishes all things
and does not demand allegiance.

Since it makes no demands for itself,
it can seem to be of small regard.
Yet as all things return to it of their own accord,
without being commanded, it can truly be regarded Great.
It is only because it does not claim to be Great
That it is able to achieve such Greatness.

35

Whoever holds firmly to following the Tao
Will draw all the World to herself.
She may go anywhere and not be afraid,
Finding only safety, balance, and peace.

Music and good food lure passers-by
But words about the Tao
Seem bland and flavorless to them.

Look, and it cannot be seen.
Listen, and it cannot be heard.
Use it, and it cannot be exhausted.

36

What you want shrunk
Must first be allowed to expand.

What you want weakened
Must first be strengthened.

What you want destroyed
Must first be allowed to flourish.

That which you want to take
Must first be given.

Seeing this is an understanding of the subtle.

What is soft and weak overcomes what is hard and strong.

Just as a fish should keep to deep waters,
So a country's weapons should be kept out of sight,
so as not to tempt people.

37

The Tao never "acts"
Yet nothing is left undone.

If the governments and leaders would keep it
All things would of their own accord be transformed.

Should desires arise from transformation
I shall influence them through silent simplicity.
Silent simplicity involves being free from desires.

When you are without desire you are content
And all the World is at peace.

38

A truly good person does not try to be good,
Therefore is he able to be good.

Another person tries to be good,
And finds that he cannot.

A good person does not act, nor has any reason to.
Another person is always doing
because he thinks he has to.

A humanitarian acts from the heart.
A politician acts, but he has ulterior motives.
When a legalist acts and gets no response,
He rolls up his sleeves and uses force.

Therefore, when the Tao is lost,
Remember that there is still goodness.
When goodness is lost, there is still kindness.
When kindness is lost, there is still the law.
When the law is lost, there is still politeness.
Politeness is the thin edge of loyalty and trust,
And is the beginning of chaos.

We need those who try to direct society
About as much as the Tao needs a flower
to make it attractive.
They mark the beginnings of stupidity.

The Sage concerns herself with causes,
Not symptoms
And focuses on the Tao, not the silly flower.
Forget the flower, follow the Tao instead.

39

People of ancient times possessed oneness.
The sky attained oneness and so became clear.
Earth attained oneness and so found peace.
The Spirit attains oneness and so is replenished.
The Valleys attained oneness and so became full.
All things attain oneness and they flourish.
The ancient leaders attained oneness
And so became examples for all the world.

All of this is achieved by oneness.

Without oneness, the sky would crack
The Earth explode
The Spirit exhaust
The Valley deplete
Leaders would certainly fall
And all life perish.

Therefore the Great recognizes the Small as its root.
The High takes the Low as its foundation.
Leaders refer to themselves as orphans and widows.
Is this not grounding oneself in humility?

Therefore the highest renown is no renown.
We do not want to glitter like jewels.
We do not want to be hard as stone.

40

Returning is the movement of the Tao.
Yielding is the way of the Tao.
All things in the world are born of existence.
Existence is born of non-existence.

41

When wise people hear about the Tao
They follow it carefully.
When ordinary people hear about the Tao
They can take it or leave it.
When foolish people hear about the Tao
They laugh out loud.
If they didn't laugh out loud, it wouldn't be the Tao!

Therefore it is said:
The path into light seems dark.
The way ahead seems to go backwards.
The path into peace seems rough.
The greatest good seems to us empty.
True purity seems stained.
The best efforts seem inadequate.
Appropriate caution seems like cowardice.
True essence seems violated.
The truly square bears no corners.
Sound vessels take time to build.
Celestial music is seldom paid much heed.
The ultimate image is impossible to capture.

The Tao is hidden and nameless
Yet it is the Tao alone that nourishes
and completes all things.

42

The Tao gives birth to one.
One gives birth to two.
Two gives birth to three,
And three gives birth to all things.

All things carry Yin and embrace Yang
Desiring nothing and finding harmony.

All people hate loneliness and poverty
Though they are the noblest of states.

So in losing, much is gained,
And in gaining, much is lost.

What others have taught, I also teach:

"The violent shall die with violence."

This is my primary teaching.

43

The softest thing in the World
Overcomes the hardest thing in the World.
That which is without substance can enter
even where there is no space.

Therefore I know the value of non-action.

Teaching without words
And benefit without actions
There are few in the World who can grasp it.

44

Fame or self: which is more important?

Your possessions or your person: which is worth more to you?

Gain or loss: which is worse?

Therefore, to be obsessed with "things" is a great waste,
The more you gain, the greater your loss.

> Being content with what you have been given,
> You can avoid disgrace.
> Knowing when to stop,
> You will avoid danger.
> That way you can live a long and happy life.

45

True perfection seems flawed
Yet its usefulness is never exhausted.

True fulfillment seems empty
Yet its usefulness is infinite.

True straightness seems crooked.
Great skill appears easy.
Great eloquence sounds awkward.

Cold overcomes heat.
Tranquility conquers agitation.
Purity and stillness is the universal ideal.

46

When the World keeps to the Tao
Strong horses are best used to manufacture manure.
When the World forgets the Tao
War horses are bred outside the city.

There is no greater curse than discontent.
Nothing breeds trouble like greed.
Only one who is content with what is enough
will be content always.

47

Without going outside,
You can know the whole world.
Without looking out the window,
You can know Heaven's Way.

The further out you seek
The less you understand.

Therefore, the Sage
Knows without needing to travel,
Understands without needing to see,
Accomplishes without "doing."

48

To pursue learning is to grow a little more every day.
To pursue the Tao is to desire a little less every day.
      Desire less and less
      Until you arrive at "not-doing."
When you practice "not-doing," nothing is left undone.

If you want to have the whole world, have nothing.
If you are always busy doing something,
you cannot enjoy the world.

49

The Sage's heart is not set in stone.
She is as sensitive to the people's feelings as to her own.

She says, "To people who are good, I am good.
And to people who are not good?
I am good to them, too."
This is true goodness.

"People who are trustworthy, I trust.
And people who are not trustworthy, I also trust."
This is real trust.

The Sage who leads harmoniously considers the mind of
her people as well as her own.
They look to her anxiously.
They are like her own children.

50

From birth to death,
Three people out of ten are celebrators of Life.
Three people out of ten are advocates of Death.
The rest simply move numbly from cradle to grave.
Why is this?

Because they are overly protective of this life.

It is said that one who knows how to protect his life can
walk freely without fear of the wild buffalo or tiger.
He may meet an army bravely with neither sword nor shield.
For the buffalo will find no place to sink its horns,
The tiger finds no place to dig his claws,
Weapons find no soft spot to pierce.
Why?

Because there is no place for death in him.

51

The Tao gives birth to all things.
Nature's goodness nurtures them.
Matter forms them.
Environment shapes them.
Therefore, all things cannot help but to
respect the Tao and treasure goodness.
Respect for the Tao and the treasuring of goodness are not
demanded of them, they do it naturally.

So, the Tao gives birth;
Nature's goodness nurtures them,
grows them, raises them and enables them to mature,
ripens them, nourishes and shelters them.

The Tao gives birth, but does not possess;
Acts, but does not take credit;
Guides, but does not control.

This is the mystery of goodness.

52

The World has an origin
Which we may regard as the Mother of the Universe.
Knowing the Mother, we can also come to know
her children.
Knowing the children, return and hold fast to the Mother.
Doing this, you will not meet with danger
your whole life long.

> Close your mouth
> Go easy on the senses
> And life will not be so hard.

> If you spend your life filling your senses
> And rushing around "doing" things
> You will be beyond hope.

To concern yourself with the beautiful and small
is true wisdom.
To foster gentleness is true strength.
Choose to do what is wise and return to wisdom.
Then you will avoid life's troubles.
This is called practicing consistency.

53

If I possess even a little wisdom
Then while I walk in the light of the Tao
My only fear is that I'll fall into "doing."
The path of the Tao is obvious and simple,
But most people prefer to take short-cuts.

The courts of law are far from the people's hearts.
    The fields are full of weeds,
    And the storehouses are empty.

But look, here are officials in elegant apparel
carrying sharp swords
Eating and drinking until they are bloated,
Possessed of such wealth that they could never use it all.

    I call this positively criminal.
    It is not the way of the Tao.

54

One who is well grounded will not be uprooted.
One who has a firm embrace will not let go.
His descendants will faithfully carry on his tradition.

Cultivate these things in yourself
And you will have true goodness.
Cultivate these in your family
And goodness will increase.
Cultivate these in your community
And goodness will catch on.
Cultivate these in your nation
And goodness will overflow!
Cultivate these in the World
And goodness will fill the Universe.

And so, let the self examine the self.
Let the family consider the family.
Let the community examine the community.
Let the nation evaluate the nation.
Let the World contemplate the World.

How do I know the World is like this?
Through these:

Grounding and embracing.

55

One who is filled with goodness is like
a freshly-born infant.
Wasps, scorpions, and snakes will not bite her.
Wild beasts will not attack her,
nor will birds of prey pounce on her.
Her bones may be fragile and her skin soft,
But her grasp is firm.
She does not recognize the union of male and female
For she knows it only as an undivided whole.
This is the essence of perfection.
She can howl all day and not get hoarse.
This is perfect harmony.

> Knowing harmony is faithfulness.
> Knowing faithfulness is salvation.

Trying to extend one's life-span is dangerous and unnatural.
To manipulate one's energy with the mind is a powerful thing
But whoever possesses such strength invariably grows old
and withers.

> This is not the way of the Tao.
> All those who do not follow the Tao will come
> to an early end.

56

Those who know, do not speak.
Those who speak, do not know.

So shut your mouth
Guard your senses
Blunt your sharpness
Untangle your affairs
Soften your glare
Be one with all dust.
This is the mystery of union.

You cannot approach it
Yet you cannot escape it.
You cannot benefit it
Yet you cannot harm it.
You cannot bestow any honor on it
Yet you cannot rob it of its dignity.
That is why the whole Universe reveres it.

57

As a leader, lead properly.
Don't resort to force in the usual ways.
Win the World by "not-doing."
How do I know to do this?

Listen, the more laws and prohibitions there are
The poorer the people become.
The more dreadful weapons you have
The more chaotic the state of the nation.
The more clever and advanced your knowledge
The stranger things become.
The more commandments and regulations you have
The more thieves there are.

Therefore the Sage who leads says:
"I practice 'not-doing' and the people transform themselves.
I enjoy peace and the people correct themselves.
I stay out of their business affairs and the people prosper.
I have no desires and the people, all by themselves,
become simple and honest."

58

When a government is unobtrusive
The people are simple and honest.
When a government is suspicious and strict
The people are discontented and sneaky.

Blessings are rooted in misery.
Misery lurks behind blessing.
Where does it ever end?

There is no such thing as "normal."
What seems normal is only an illusion,
And what seems good is finally revealed to be monstrous.
The people's confusion has lasted a very long time.

Therefore the Sage is honest, but not judgmental
Strong, but not injurious to others
Straightforward, but not reckless
Bright, but not blinding.

59

In leading people and serving Heaven
There is nothing better than moderation.
In moderation, one is already following the Tao.
When one follows the Tao, great goodness is abundant.
When great goodness is in abundance,
There is nothing that cannot be overcome.
When there is nothing that cannot be overcome
Then there are no limits.
Having no limits, one can certainly govern a country.
If you know the country's Mother, you will long endure.

I call this having deep roots and a firm stalk.
This is the Way of long life and great insight.

60

Govern a big country as you would fry a small fish.

Approach the world with the Tao and evil will have no power.
Not that evil has no power, but it will not harm people.

Not that evil is not harmful,
but the Sage is dedicated to not harming people—even evil people.
When no one hurts another,
all will eventually return to the good.

61

A great country is like a low-lying lake where many rivers converge;
A focal point for the Earth, the feminine Spirit of the World.
The female always overcomes the male by stillness.
Stillness is the lowest position.

> Therefore a big country,
> By placing itself below a smaller country
> Will win the smaller country.

> And a small country,
> By placing itself below a larger country
> Will gain the large country.

> Therefore, by being humble, one gains
> And the other, being humble already, also gains.

> A great country needs to embrace the lowly.
> The small country needs to serve others.
> Thus, both needs are satisfied
> And each gets what it wants.

Remember, the great country should always humble itself.

62

The Tao is the bosom of the Universe
It is the good person's treasure
And the bad person's refuge.

Flattery may buy one's position
And good deeds can win people over
But if one's heart is not pure
That is all the more reason to cling to the Tao!

Therefore when a king is coronated,
Crowned in ceremony,
Presented with gifts of rare value,
And escorted in luxury,
All these things pale when compared to the humble gift
of the Tao, offered in silence.

Why did the Sages of old value the Tao so much?
Because when you seek, you find
And when you sin, you are forgiven.

That is why the Tao is the greatest treasure of the Universe.

63

Do without "doing."
Work without forcing.
Taste without seasonings.
Recognize the Great in the small,
And the many in the few.

Repay hatred with kindness.

Deal with the difficult while it is still easy.
Begin great works while they are small.
Certainly the Earth does difficult work with ease,
And accomplishes great affairs from small beginnings.
So, the Sage, by not striving for greatness,
Achieves greatness.

A person who makes promises lightly
Is not regarded as trustworthy.

If you think everything is easy,
You will find only difficulty.
That is why the Sage considers all things difficult
And finds nothing too difficult in the end.

64

What is at rest is easy to maintain.
What has not yet happened is easy to plan.
That which is fragile is easily shattered
That which is tiny is easily scattered.

> Correct problems before they occur.
> Intervene before chaos erupts.

A tree too big around to hug is produced from a tiny sprout.
A nine-story tower begins with a mound of dirt.
A thousand-mile journey begins with your own two feet.

> Whoever tries will fail.
> Whoever clutches, loses.

> Therefore the Sage, not trying, cannot fail
> Not clutching, she cannot lose.

> When people try,
> they usually fail just on the brink of success.
> If one is as cautious at the outset as at the end,
> One cannot fail.

Therefore the Sage desires nothing so much
as to be desireless.
She does not value rare and expensive goods.
She unlearns what she was once taught
And helps the people regain what they have lost;
To help every being assume its natural way of being,
And not dare to force anything.

65

In ancient times those who followed the Tao
Did not try to educate the people.
They chose to let them be.

The reason people become hard to govern
Is that they think they know it all.
So, if a leader tries to lead through cleverness,
He is nothing but a liability.
But if a leader leads, not through cleverness,
but through goodness, this is a blessing to all.

To be always conscious of the Great Pattern
is a spiritual virtue.

Spiritual virtue is awesome and infinite
And it leads all things back to their Source.
Then there emerges the Great Harmony.

66

Rivers and the sea are able to rule the streams
of a hundred valleys.
Because they are good at taking the lower position,
The streams of a hundred valleys run to them.

Therefore, if you want to rule effectively over people
You must surely speak as if below them.
If you want to lead well,
You must surely walk behind them.

That way when the Sage takes a position of power
The people will not feel oppressed.
And when the Sage leads
The people will not think he is in the way.

Therefore the whole world joyfully praises him
and does not tire of him.

Because he refuses to compete,
The world cannot compete with him.

67

Everyone says this Tao of mine is great and nebulous.
So great, in fact, that it is too nebulous to be of any use.

I have three treasures that I hold and cherish:
One is called "compassion"
Another is called "moderation"
And the third is called "daring not to compete."

With compassion, one is able to be brave.
With moderation, one has enough to be generous with others.
Without competition, one is fit to lead.

Nowadays people don't bother with compassion
But just try to be brave.
They scoff at moderation
And find they have little enough for themselves.
They step on people in their rush to be first—
This is death!

One who is compassionate in warfare is victorious
And in defense he holds fast.
When Heaven moves to save someone
It protects him through compassion.

68

The best soldier is not violent.
The best fighter is not driven by anger.
The true conqueror wins without confrontation.
The best employer is humble before his employees.

I say there is much good in not competing.
I call it using the power of the people.
This is known as being in tune with Heaven,
Like the Sages of old.

69

The military has a saying:

> "I would rather be passive, like a guest
> than aggressive, like a host.
> I would rather retreat a foot
> than advance an inch."

> This is called going forward without instigating,
> Engaging without force
> Defense without hatred
> Victory without weapons.

There is no greater calamity than underestimating the enemy.
If I take my enemy too lightly, I am in danger of losing my
compassion, moderation, and non-competitive spirit.

So, when two armies confront each other
Victory will go to them that grieve.

70

My words are very easy to understand
And very easy to practice.
Yet the World is not able to understand
Nor able to put them into practice.

My words speak of the primal.
My deeds are but service.
Unless people understand this
They won't understand me.
And since so few understand me,
Then such understanding is rare and valuable indeed.

Therefore the Sage wears common clothes
And hides his treasures only in his heart.

71

She who knows that she does not know is the best off.
He who pretends to know but doesn't is ill.

Only someone who realizes he is ill can become whole.
The Sage is not ill because she recognizes
this illness as illness,
Therefore she is not ill.

72

When people lose their fear of power
Then great power has indeed arrived.

Do not intrude on the people's material living.
Do not despise their spiritual lives, either.
If you respect them, you will be respected.

Therefore the Sage knows himself,
but he is not opinionated.
He loves himself, but he is not arrogant.

He lets go of conceit and opinion,
and embraces self-knowledge and love.

73

A soldier who has the courage to fight
will eventually be killed.
But one who has the courage not to fight will live.

In these two, one is good and the other harmful.
Who knows why Heaven allows some things to happen?
Even the Sage is stumped sometimes.

The Way of Heaven
Does not compete, but is good at winning;
Does not speak, yet always responds;
Does not demand, but is usually obeyed;
Seems chaotic, but unfolds a most excellent plan.

> Heaven's net is cast wide
> And though its meshes are loose,
> Nothing is ever lost.

74

If people do not fear death
How can you threaten them with it?

If people live in constant fear of death,
Because those who break the law are seized and killed,
Who would dare to break the law?

There has always been an official executioner.
If you take the law into your own hands
And try to take his place,
It is like trying to take the place of a master carpenter
In which case you would probably hurt your hands.

75

The people are starving because their leaders
eat up all their money in taxes.
And so, they are hungry.

The people are rebellious
because their leaders are intrusive.
And so, they protest.

The people make light of death because their leaders
live so well at their expense.
And so, they expect death.

Therefore, it seems that one who does not grasp this life
too tightly is better off than one who clings.

76

When people are alive they are soft and weak.
At their death they are hard and rigid.

All young things, including grass and trees
Are soft and frail.
At their death they are withered and dry.

So, all that are hard and rigid take the company of death.
Those who are soft and weak take the company of life.

Therefore, powerful weapons will not succeed
(Remember that strong and tall trees
are the ones that are cut down).

The strong and rigid are broken and laid low.
The soft and weak will always overcome.

77

The Tao of Heaven is like the stringing of a bow.
The high is pressed down and the low is raised up.
The string that is too long is shortened
and the string that is too short is added to.

Heaven's Way is to take from what has too much
And give it to what does not have enough.
This is not the way of men, however,
for they take from those who have little
to increase the wealth of the rich.

So who is it that has too much
and offers it to a needy World?
Only someone who knows the Tao.

Therefore, the Sage works anonymously.
She achieves great things
but does not wait around for praise.
She does not want her talents to attract attention to her.

78

In the whole World nothing is softer or weaker than water.
And yet even those who succeed when attacking
the hard and the strong cannot overcome it
Because nothing can harm it.
The weak overcomes the strong.
The soft conquers the hard.

    No one in the World can deny this
    Yet no one seems to know how to put it into practice.

Therefore the Sage says
"One who accepts a people's shame is qualified to rule it.
One who embraces a condemned people
is called the king of the Universe."

    True words seem paradoxical.

79

When enemies are reconciled, some resentment invariably remains.
How can this be healed?

> Therefore the Sage makes good on his half of the deal
> And demands nothing of others.

> One who is truly good will keep his promise.
> One who is not good will take what he can.

> Heaven doesn't choose sides
> It is always with the good people.

80

It is best to have small communities with few people.
And although they have goods and equipment in abundance
few of them are even used.
They have great love of life,
and are content to be right where they are.
And although they have boats and carriages,
there is no place they particularly want to go.
And although they have access to weapons and machineries
of war, they have no desire to show them off.

> Let people return to simplicity,
> working with their own hands.
> Then they will find joy in their food
> Beauty in their simple clothes
> Peace in their living
> Fulfillment in their traditions.

And although they live within sight of neighboring states
And their roosters and dogs are heard by one another
The people are content to grow old and die
Without having gone to see their neighbor states.

81

True words are not beautiful.
Beautiful words are not true.

Good people do not argue.
Argumentative people are not good.

The wise are not necessarily well-educated.
The well-educated are not necessarily wise.

The Sage does not hoard things.
The more she does for others
The more she finds she has.
The more she gives to others
The more she finds she gains.

Heaven's Way is to nourish, not to harm.
The Sage's Way is to work, yet not compete.

ABOUT THE TRANSLATION

This version of the *Tao Te Ching* was translated from the Chinese text, and is based on Dr. Yi Wu's Chinese/English interlinear, *The Book of Lao Tzu (The Tao Te Ching)*, published by Great Learning Publishing in 1989, and was revised under guidance from Dr. Wu.

ABOUT THE TRANSLATOR

JOHN R. MABRY, PHD studied Chinese at the California Institute of Integral Studies. He holds a doctorate in world religions, and teaches interfaith theology at the Chaplaincy Institute for Arts and Interfaith Ministry in Berkeley, CA.

He also serves as co-pastor of Grace North Church, a progressive liturgical community. Former editor of *Creation Spirituality* magazine and *Presence: An International Journal of Spiritual Direction*, he is currently the managine editor of the *Pacific Church News*.

Other books by John Mabry include *God As Nature Sees God: a Christian Reading of the Tao Te Ching* and *Heretics, Mystics & Misfits*, both available in Apocryphile Press editions.

Contact John at jmabry@apocryphile.org or visit his website: www.apocryphile.org/jrm/

www.ingramcontent.com/pod-product-compliance
Lightning Source LLC
Chambersburg PA
CBHW030516100426
42813CB00001B/57

*9 7 8 1 9 5 5 8 2 1 3 3 9 *